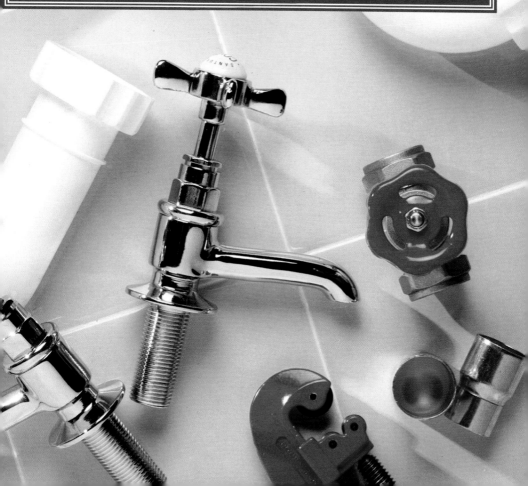

Made Simple

PLUMBING

David Holloway

Made Simple

PLUMBING

David Holloway

Bloomsbury Books
London

Made Simple
PLUMBING

Page 2: A fully fitted 'all mod con' kitchen made possible by advances in plumbing.

This edition published in 1994 by Bloomsbury Books,
an imprint of The Godfrey Cave Group,
42 Bloomsbury Street, London. WC1B 3QJ

Under license from Harlaxton Publishing Limited
2 Avenue Road, Grantham, Lincolnshire, NG31 6TA, United Kingdom.
A member of the Weldon International Group of Companies.

Copyright © 1994 Harlaxton Publishing Limited
Copyright Design © 1994 Harlaxton Publishing Limited

Publisher: Robin Burgess
Design and Coordination: Rachel Rush
Editing: Martyn Hocking
Illustrator: Jane Pickering, Linden Artists
Photography: Chris Allen, Forum Advertising Limited
Typesetting: Seller's, Grantham
Colour Reproduction: GA Graphics, Stamford
Printing: Imago, Singapore

British Library Cataloguing-in-Publication data.
A catalogue record for this book is available from the British Library.
Title: Made Simple - PLUMBING
ISBN: 1-85471-342-6

Made Simple

CONTENTS

To many people plumbing is a mystery. Turn the taps on and cold water comes out of one and hot out of the other; pull the plug out or flush the loo and water disappears. Everything is fine – until, that is, something goes wrong.

Understanding how your plumbing system works, learning about the tools, techniques and materials that you need, will help you to prevent problems, and cope with problems as they occur. It will also allow you to make additions and alterations to your plumbing system – or to your central heating system – to improve and upgrade them.

For the amateur, plumbing has never been easier. For a start, the tools, materials and equipment you need are now widely accessible with the mushrooming growth of the do-it-yourself superstores. But advances in the materials, especially with the advent of plastic plumbing pipe and push-fit fittings, has made the actual joining of pipe much easier. No longer is there a need to be able to work with lead supply pipe (the word 'plumber' comes from the Latin *plumbum* meaning 'lead'); no longer is there a need to work with cast iron for outside soil pipes. The myth and the magic has in some part been removed.

RULES AND REGULATIONS

The main rules affecting plumbing work in the home are the Water Bylaws issued by your local water company. Apart from some minor local differences, these are standard.

Bylaws are to prevent waste, undue consumption, misuse or contamination of the mains water supply. Many of the regulations are regarding back-siphonage – to prevent water from your house returning to the mains supply. You are required by law to give notice of five working days to your Water Company if you intend to fit a bidet, a flushing cistern, a hose union tap or any appliance through which water could contaminate the mains supply.

Prosecutions are rare but the penalties for contravening the water bylaws can be steep – and will mount daily until you correct the fault. Bylaws represent good plumbing practice and you should get a copy from your local Water Company (they are usually free).

Water Bylaws cover only the supply side of plumbing; the waste and soil is covered by the Building Regulations administered by your local council. You should find out something about what the Regulations say in order that you do not contravene them.

Minor alterations and replacements are not affected, but to do work which will affect the underground drains, you should inform the Building Control Department of your local council, who will normally be very helpful.

Installing gas central heating is covered by the Gas Safety (Installation and Use) Regulations which make it illegal to do any of the gas fitting work yourself. Only a gas-fitter or plumber registered with CORGI (Council for Registered Gas Installers) may do the work.

Any electrical work is covered by the IEE Wiring Regulations, incorporated in British Standard BS 7671. Although not mandatory in England and Wales, in Scotland, they are part of the Building Regulations and so have the force of law.

OPPOSITE: Regular repairs and maintenance keep the water flowing in a busy kitchen.

Made Simple
PLUMBING BASICS

There is just one water supply to the home – cold water from the Water Company mains.

Somewhere inside the house, there will be a system for heating the water to provide the domestic hot water (DHW) which comes out of the taps and, usually, another system for heating water for circulating around radiators to provide central heating.

A systems of pipes carries cold water, hot water, and central heating water around the house. Another system of (larger) pipes carries the waste water away from basins, sinks, baths and WCs. These are connected to the soil system which runs into underground drains.

COLD WATER SYSTEMS

In all homes connected to mains water, the supply comes via a branch pipe from the water main in the street. Just outside the property boundary there is a stopcock under a metal cover, so that the Water Company can isolate the supply. From there the service pipe runs into the house under the floorboards to the householder's stopcock, usually situated under the kitchen sink, or in older houses, just inside the front door.

A pipe, called the rising main, runs through the house from the householder's stopcock with a branch pipe leading to the kitchen sink cold tap – to provide fresh water for drinking and cooking – and a draincock just above the stopcock – for draining down the system.

1: DIRECT SYSTEM – All the other cold taps in the house – usually the bathroom basin and bath – plus the WC are fed directly from this rising main.

2: INDIRECT SYSTEM – The rising main feeds a large (50 gallons/227 litres) cold water cistern (3) in the loft which in turn feeds the cold taps and WCs.

1

3

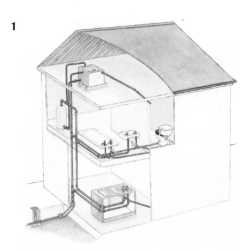
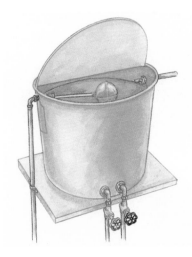

The flow of water into the cistern is controlled by a ballvalve – which shuts off when the water reaches a certain level – and an overflow pipe which leads to the outside and drains off excess water if it rises too high or the ballvalve fails. A gatevalve on the pipe leading out of the cistern allows the cold taps and WC to be isolated for maintenance without having to drain the cistern down.

The original idea of the cold water cistern was to provide cold water storage for the home in the event of mains failure. Prolonged mains failure is rare these days and having a cistern has many disadvantages. The water inside can become contaminated or it can freeze (particularly now that loft spaces are well insulated), which could be disastrous.

HOT WATER SYSTEMS

By far the most common system for heating domestic hot water is a hot water cylinder. It is usually made of copper and contains around 26 gallons/120 litres of water.

An indirect cylinder (4) is fed from the main cold water cistern or, where the cold water system is 'direct', by its own mains-fed cold water cistern, mounted either in the loft or just above the hot water cylinder.

The cold feed pipe to the cylinder enters at the bottom, while the pipe which feeds the hot water taps emerges from the top of the cylinder, because hot water rises.

A third pipe – the safety open vent – is attached to the pipe leading out of the top of the cylinder and loops back to the cistern, and is twisted into a downwards-pointing position. This allows air and steam to escape should the system overheat – water expands as it heats up affecting the cold feed pipe.

A hot water cylinder can be heated either by an electric immersion heater or by a sealed, coiled pipe which carries water heated by the boiler. Except in very old (now outmoded) systems, the water from the boiler and the water inside the cylinder do not mix.

2

4

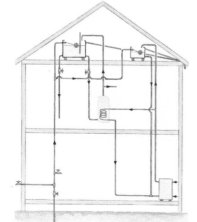
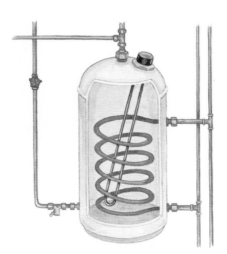

An alternative method of heating the hot water is to have a gas-fired multipoint heater. Cold water passes through this and is heated almost instantly by a gas burner. It then circulates to all the hot water taps in the house. A recent development is the combination boiler which combines the function of a multipoint heater and a central heating boiler. The advantages of both are that there is a constant supply of hot water and that it is possible to get rid of the cold water cistern in the loft (provided the cold water supply is direct); the disadvantage is that the water flow rate is generally slower than a cistern-fed system, meaning that baths take longer to fill.

The latest type of hot water system is the unvented hot water storage system, in which a special hot water cylinder is fed direct from the rising main. An expansion vessel allows for expansion and safety valves allow air and steam to escape. This type of system can only be installed by a suitably qualified plumber.

RIGHT:
A multipoint gas fired combination central heating boiler.

WASTE SYSTEMS

The dirty water from baths, basins and sinks is taken away by waste pipes, which lead to the main soil pipe. All these pipes must be fitted with a water-filled trap – fitted immediately after the bath, basin or sink – which prevents smells from the drains getting back into the house. There are different designs of trap, but they all perform the same job.

In older houses, the waste from the bath and basins is fed into a hopper head connected to the top of the soil pipe, which in turn leads into the gully into which the waste pipe from the kitchen sink also runs. The gully leads to the underground drains.

A WC or bidet must also contain a water-filled trap (built into the WC pan) and the waste pipe goes directly to the soil pipe. In older (two-pipe) systems WCs have their own soil pipe which is separate from the soil pipe for baths and basins.

1: A MODERN SYSTEM – is single-stack with WC and bidet waste fed into the same pipe as the bath and basin wastes; the layout ensures the two wastes are kept separate until they are safely inside the pipe. Many modern single-stack systems may have the main soil pipe inside the house, but this is no longer a requirement of the Building Regulations. Underground, the wastes from the soil pipes and kitchen sink gully are removed by the drains either to the main sewer or, in rural properties, to a cesspool or a septic tank.

2: A CESSPOOL – is simply a storage tank which needs to be emptied regularly.

3: A SEPTIC TANK – is a miniature sewage works, in which bacteriological action separates the waste into a harmless liquid and a sludge. The sludge needs removing about once a year. When working well, septic tanks are very effective, but you need to be careful to keep them clean – especially being careful how you use bleach, disinfectant and detergents, which can kill the bacteria.

1

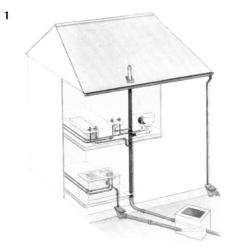

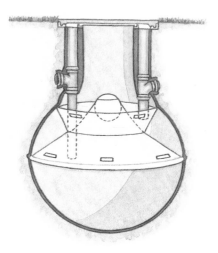

3

Made Simple
TOOLS, MATERIALS
AND TECHNIQUES

Lead was the main material used in plumbing but gradually new concepts and regulations have led to the introduction of new materials and techniques.

PLUMBING MATERIALS

In some houses, you may need to join the older 'imperial' sizes of pipe to the now current metric sizes. To do this you will need the appropriate adaptor which can usually only be supplied by specialist plumbing suppliers.

For making capillary fittings you will need an adaptor when joining 22mm pipe to old 3_4in pipe, or with 15mm pipe to old 1_2in pipe, and with 28mm pipe to old 1in pipe.

When using compression fittings you do not need an adaptor for joining 15mm to 1_2in or 28mm to 1in pipe.

BELOW: 1 - Compression Fittings
      2 - Capillary fittings 'Yorkshire'
      3 - Capillary fittings 'End-feed'

4- Olives
5 - Copper tube 15mm
6- Copper tube 22mm
7 - Solder

PIPES AND FITTINGS

For hot and cold water supply pipes, the most common material is copper – lead is not used in new installations and has largely been replaced in older installations.

There are two main pipe sizes. For pipes under mains pressure, and the final feed pipes to basins, WCs and radiators 15mm is used.

The supply pipes to bath taps, the cold supply pipe to the hot water cylinder, the open vent pipe and the main central heating pipe runs use 22mm.

Copper pipe is mainly joined in one of two ways.

1: COMPRESSION FITTINGS – nuts on the ends of the fittings compress flat brass rings – called 'olives' – to make a seal. Compression fittings have the advantage that they allow some adjustment of the pipe within the fitting by loosening the nut which, when making complicated pipe runs with lots of corners, is helpful.

2: CAPILLARY FITTINGS – solder is heated to flow between the pipe and the fitting to make the seal. There are two types of capillary fitting.
End-feed fittings, which contain no solder and need to have the solder added as the fitting is heated up.
Solder-ring or 'Yorkshire' fittings, which have solder already contained within the end bulge of the fitting.
Capillary fittings are cheaper and neater, but have the disadvantage that there is a skill required to make the join – which can be difficult to achieve.

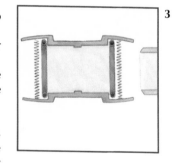

3: PUSH-FIT PLASTIC FITTINGS – are used largely for various drainage pipe systems and over flows. Some have to be made using a solvent adhesive although increasingly many drainage systems use built-in rubber seals. These can be expensive but they are the easiest of all to make and allow the pipe to be turned inside the fitting even after the joint has been made.
Some recently developed push-fit accessory fittings for pressure pipes are expensive because of the internal metal ferrels.

Plastic has been the main material used for drainage services for some time. Some have to be made using a solvent adhesive although increasingly many drainage systems use built-in rubber seals. Increasingly the material used for supply plumbing is also plastic.

Rigid plastic pipes and fittings used for supply services have the advantage that they are very cheap, but the disadvantage that they are not easy to make as the pipes have to be 'solvent-welded'.

Plastic pipes have the major advantage that they come in long lengths. This allows pipe runs to be made with virtually no fittings and allows the pipe to be run through holes cut in the centre of joists rather than through notches cut in the top edge. The plastic fittings are obtrusive because of their bulk and some push-fittings with internal metal ferrels expensive.

Plastic pipes need to be fitted with adequate space for expansion, especially if used for – or in the vicinity of –-hot water or central heating as plastic pipe tends to sag.

Plastic pipe is widely used for waste and soil pipes and sometimes for underground drains, where modern flexible push-fit connectors have made joining traditional under-ground clay pipes much easier.

OPPOSITE: Full-size pipe cutters (1) have a pointed reamer at one end for removing the burr made inside the pipe. When using a hacksaw (2), you will need to file (3) both the inside and outside of the pipe. When using capillary fittings the ends of copper pipe must be cleaned with wire wool (4).

BELOW: Modern plastic fittings and pipe.

PLUMBING TOOLS AND TECHNIQUES

The main techniques needed are how to cut, bend and join pipes and how to make screwed connections.

You must also be able to do basic building work – lifting floorboards, making small, medium and large holes in walls, cutting notches and holes in joists, making good damage to plaster – and have the right tools for these jobs.

2

CUTTING PIPE

1 Semi-flexible plastic pipe is easy to cut. All you need is a pair of secateurs (5) – either special or garden secateurs.

2 Rigid plastic piping including waste pipe is cut with a fine-toothed hacksaw. On large pipes, wrap a piece of paper around the pipe to ensure the cut remains square.

3

3 For copper pipe, the best tool to use is a pipe cutter (1), which has a hardened steel wheel which is progressively advanced into the pipe. Small circular versions (6) can be used close to walls, but sometimes you will need to resort to using a hacksaw.

BENDING PIPE

1

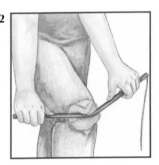

2

3

S ometimes it is necessary to bend copper pipe in a gentle curve to go around corners or to fit round another pipe.
Semi-flexible plastic pipe can be bent without the use of tools – rigid plastic pipe cannot be bent at all.

To bend small bore copper pipe

1 Use a pipe-bending spring. Tie a length of string to the loop at the end of the spring. Insert the spring into the pipe and position it either side of the bend position.

2 Ensure that you hold the pipe within the length of the spring. Place a sponge block between your knee and the pipe as you bend the pipe – it will distort without the spring.

3 For deep bends retrieve the spring using the string, or use a screw driver as shown if it cannot be removed easily.

Short lengths of hand-bendable, flexible, copper pipe can be brought which are useful for awkward connections – such as under a basin or behind a bath. These must not be used for connecting shower pumps – special connectors are available for this – nor in central heating systems.

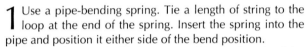

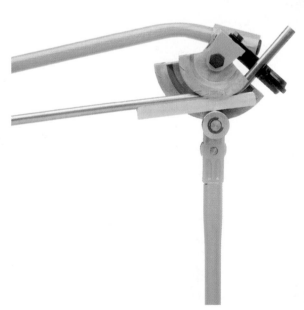

RIGHT: For large bore pipes hire or buy a pipe-bending machine.

USING FITTINGS

A good selection of spanners (preferably adjustable ones) is essential for working on compression fittings.

Plumber's wrenches with serrated jaws are designed to turn iron pipes – they will damage the surface of nuts.

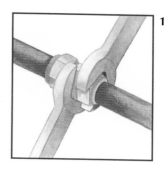

Using compression fittings

1 Place the components in sequence on the pipe with the 'olives' in position. Always use a spanner to turn the nut and a second to hold the fitting.

Using capillary fittings

2 Copper pipe ends must be scrupulously clean with flux applied to both the pipes and the inside of the fitting.

A gas blowtorch is the most convenient tool. Use a flame-resistant mat to protect flammable materials such as floorboards. Pipe-soldering tongs are safer to use in some situations though they take longer.

With the fitting in place apply heat until solder appears at the rim of a solder-ring fitting – or until a neat ring of molten solder is built around the rim with an end-feed fitting.

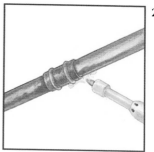

Using push-fit fittings

3 Push-fit fittings need no special tools, but it is essential to follow the instructions supplied with the fittings and to ensure that the copper inserts supplied are used with push-fit fittings on plastic piping.

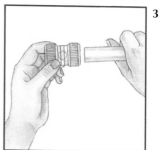

Using threaded fittings

4 In plumbing there are many threaded connections – especially on hot water cylinders and central heating boilers. It is essential that screwed joints make a perfect seal. Traditionally hemp and plumber's mastic were inserted between the male and female threads. Today, white PTFE tape – available in rolls – is used.

Wind the PTFE tape around the threads – about seven times, in a clockwise direction – so that it is forced tight into the threads as the joint is made.

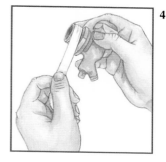

Made Simple
TROUBLESHOOTING

The first time many householders encounter the plumbing system in their home is when they have a problem.

Most plumbing problems such as dripping taps, leaks, blocked basins or sinks, noises, frozen pipes and the like can be solved relatively simply.

Although such jobs are often messy, provided that you know what you are doing and have the correct tools and equipment, they are not complicated tasks. A very few problems, such as tree roots growing into an underground drain, will need professional help to solve.

SERVICING VALVES

It is a requirement of the Water Bylaws that servicing valves be fitted to pipes leading to taps or ballvalves.

This is to make it easier to repair or replace either a tap or a ballvalve without the need to turn off the water and drain the pipe. Many of the repair jobs you need to do will involve turning off the water and draining the pipe. To avoid having to do this too often, it is a good idea, wherever possible, to fit a few in-line servicing valves.

Cut out a short length of pipe – without making the overall pipe length either longer or shorter – and replace it with an in-line servicing valve. These usually have compression fittings on either end with a small, internal, shut-off 'ball' mechanism, that can be operated by a coin or screwdriver.

RIGHT: In-line servicing valves with a shut-off mechanism.

BLOCKED SINK OR BASIN

W hen waste water is either sluggish or refuses to run away from a basin, sink, bath or shower tray.

1 The first thing to try is the trusty sink plunger or the more powerful, hand-operated force pump. Nine times out of ten, this will force the blockage out of the pipe and allow the water to run freely.

2 If plunging does not work, use a length of wire through the plug hole to work the blockage free. A plumber will use a 'snake', a long length of flexible wire with a hook on the end. You can buy one of these yourself. Pull rather than push the blockage.

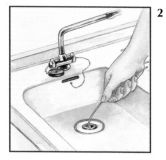

3 The next stage is to dismantle the trap. Wear rubber gloves to protect your hands and make sure you have a large bucket beneath the trap to catch the water.

4 Again, 'wiggling' the blockage with a length of wire will help. Remember to refit the trap before tidying up. Dispose of the bucket contents outside!

5 Finally, when the blockage is at least partially clear, you can use a chemical – such as caustic soda.

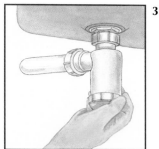

Do not use chemicals on a completely blocked sink – the plastic trap may melt – and you could end up with a bucket of toxic chemicals!

Follow the instructions to the letter and wear rubber gloves. Use a dilute solution of washing soda at monthly intervals down bath, basin and sink plug holes to help keep them free from blockages.

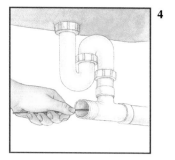

BLOCKED DRAINS

The first sign that indicates a blocked drain is usually an overflowing gully.

1 Trace the direction of the drains and the sequence of inspection chambers. Lift all the manhole covers until you find a dry inspection chamber – the blockage is between this dry one and the previous full one.

2 Remove the blockage with hired or bought drain rods. Drain rods are supplied with plunger discs for pushing the blockage out and with 'corkscrews' for dislodging it.

3 Push the drain rod into the outlet of the full inspection chamber, adding more extension rods as necessary.

Never twist the rods anticlockwise or they could unscrew underground.

4 If the blockage is in the final inspection chamber before the sewer – this is usually caused by the 'rodding arm' plug falling into the interceptor trap.

Use some stiff twisted wire, or a 'snake' to pull the plug out and then rod with the plunger disc to clean out the trap.

Underground drains should be hosed down once a year and damaged concrete haunching repaired – when small bits of haunching break off they can cause blockages.

3
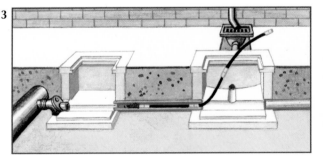

4
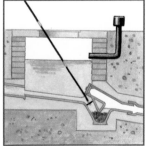

DRIPPING TAPS

A dripping or dribbling tap usually indicates, and is caused by, a failed tap-washer.

1 **Turn off the water supply** – to the tap and open the tap to let the pipe drain.

2 Remove the tap handle – and the domed tap cover on old style taps. Unscrew the large nut formed around the barrel of the tap mechanism. This comes out in one piece with the washer at the bottom – usually held in place by a small nut or flange. Replace the washer with one that is of the same size and shape as the original.

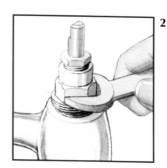

3 Before replacing the tap mechanism, inspect the brass washer seat inside the tap. If it is badly scored, it will need to be re-ground with a tap reseating tool – which you can hire – or a new nylon seat inserted. If you do not do this the new tap washer will not be effective.

4 Assembly is the reverse of dismantling – if the tap leaks from the top when the water is turned on, it could be that the O-ring seal needs to be replaced or, on older taps, that the packing has failed.

Remove the packing by unscrewing the small nut under the dome cover, pick out the old, dried-out packing and replace it with wool that is smeared with petroleum jelly.

Re-packing should also cure a tap which is stiff to operate – no more than fingertip pressure should ever be required.

LEFT: A modern tap design that does not have the the older style dome.

LEAKING OVERFLOW

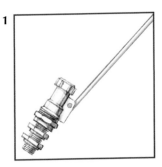

The overflow pipe from a cold water or WC cistern is a 'warning' and is meant to annoy you – so that you fix it.

It is usually a failed washer on an old-fashioned piston-operated ballvalve – dirt or grit in the mechanism.

1 It is possible to clean up and repair the washer on a piston-operated ballvalve.

2 A much better solution is to replace it with a modern diaphragm ballvalve (brass or plastic), as is required on new installations. A diaphragm ballvalve is more compact and easier to adjust, also it is much quieter in operation.

To replace or repair a ballvalve

3 **Turn off the water supply** – to the cistern at the mains or at the cold water cistern if appropriate.

4 Unscrew the nut holding the pipe to the ballvalve. The tap connector on the end of the pipe can usually be connected directly to the new ballvalve – make sure the small fibre washer which makes the seal is undamaged and in place.

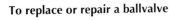
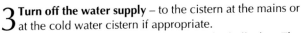

THIS PAGE: A selection of different, ball valve units in common use.

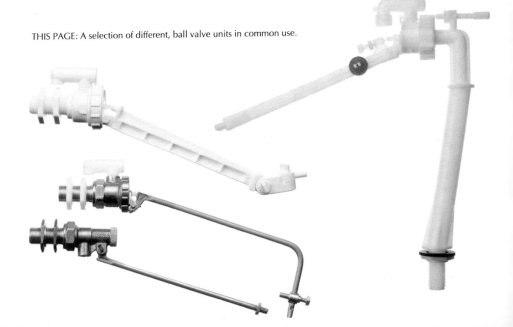

AIRLOCKS

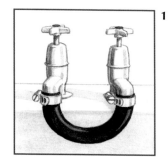

1

A n airlock is often the cause for water refusing to flow from a tap.

The usual cause is badly run pipework – especially hot water pipes that run slightly uphill from the open vent pipe connection rather than the necessary slight downward slope. Sometimes the cause is either a cold water cistern or a pipe feeding the hot water cylinder that is too small.

To cure an airlock

1 Attach one end of a pipe to a tap with mains pressure – the kitchen cold tap in an 'indirect' cold system or any cold tap in a 'direct' system – the other end of the hose to the offending tap.

2 Turn both taps full on. Only if the primary cause of the problem is cured, will the airlock be removed.

NOISES

1 CREAKING NOISES – in plumbing systems are caused by hot water and central heating pipes expanding as they warm up and rub against notches cut in flooring joists.

The solution is to raise the floorboards and slip some foam pipe insulation around the pipes where they cross the joists – sometimes the notch may need to be enlarged.

2 NOISY FILLING – of the cistern can be cured by replacing a piston-operated ballvalve with a diaphragm type (see page 22).

1

Make sure the ballvalve is the correct type – low-pressure for cistern-fed supplies and high-pressure for mains-fed supplies.

3 LOUD BANGING – in the pipes, often started when a tap is turned off, is known as 'water hammer' and is actually a shock wave passing down the pipe.

Often it can be cured by closing the mains stopcock a little to reduce the flow of water. Sometimes a replacement diaphragm ballvalve will do the trick, and occasionally you will need to change one or more tap washers.

NEXT PAGE: A modern kitchen and utility area are the plumbing nerve centre of the home.

FROZEN OR BURST PIPES

Under normal circumstances pipes will not usually freeze in houses which are occupied and heated.

If a house is left empty during the winter, ice can form in the pipes and joints which if left unattended, will 'burst' – either splitting the pipe or 'blowing' a joint apart – with disastrous results as water pours all over the house.

Defrosting a frozen pipe

1 A frozen water pipe is indicated when there is no water from a tap and it is known not to be an airlock.

This can be cured by opening the tap and using a hair-dryer to heat the pipe. Work back from the tap until the frozen blockage is reached. This will be where the pipe is exposed to the coldest temperatures – in an outhouse, in the loft or under any downstairs floorboards.

Repairing a burst pipe

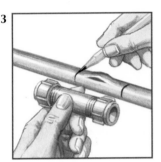

2 Purchase a burst-pipe repair coupling – an elongated compression fitting – or a repair kit. **Turn the water off** – and drain the pipe system.

A burst pipe can be dealt with immediately using a burst-pipe repair clamp without turning the water off.

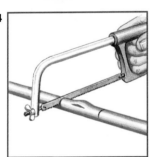

3 Mark off the burst part of the pipe to the effective length of the repair coupling.

4 Cut out the damaged pipe using a fine-cut hacksaw. File off any burrs and use wire wool to remove stain, grease or paint from around the ends of the pipe.

5 Fit the repair coupling elements in sequence ensuring that the 'olives' are correctly seated.

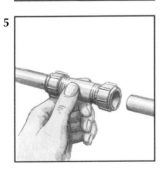

Minimise the danger of burst pipes by draining the water system before leaving a house empty in the winter. Do not drain the central heating system – add antifreeze instead.

WC FLUSH FAILURE

If a low-level WC fails to flush or is difficult to flush, the fault is usually the large clear plastic 'flapvalve' washer.
The function of this is to carry water over the inverted 'U' of the flushing mechanism to start the siphonic operation.

1 **Turn off the water supply** – to the cistern, then flush it to remove the water. Dismantle the flushing mechanism until you can get to the 'flapvalve' washer (1).

2 Replace the washer with a new one of the same size and type – if you cannot get one of exactly the same size, buy a larger one and cut it down.

3 Complete flush failure may be due to a broken link (2) which is easily replaced.

4 Difficult flushing on an old-fashioned, high-level cistern is usually due to dirt. A good clean is usually sufficient.

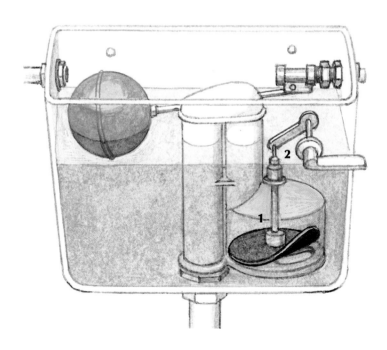

PROBLEMS WITH SCALE

I n hard water areas, water will produce scale if heated above 70°C/160°F. This is the familiar 'fur' inside kettles.

Scale can build up inside hot water pipes and cylinders, it can damage the element in hot water cylinders, and cause stains in baths, basins and sinks.

1 Minimise the formation of scale in electrically-heated hot water systems by ensuring that an immersion heater thermostat is set to no more than 60°C/140°F.

2 Scale can be a particular problem in water heaters that produce instant hot water – gas multipoints, gas sink heaters and electric showers – since the temperature of the water at the heater is much higher than 70°C/160°F.

3 A solution is to fit a polyphosphate dosing unit in the cold pipe leading to the heater. The polyphosphate – which is non-toxic – will prevent scale formation. Ensure stopcocks are fitted either side of the unit so that it can be removed for maintenance or repair.

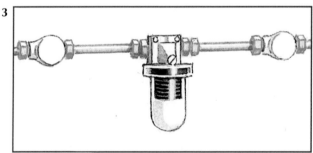

3

STIFF STOPCOCKS

If left unused for a long period, stopcocks can become very difficult (if not impossible) to turn – and you do not want to discover this when you have an emergency!

To free a stopcock, apply some heat with boiling water from a kettle then add a little penetrating oil to the spindle. Once the stopcock is free, close it half a turn from fully open to prevent it sticking again.

LEAKING PIPE JOINTS

COMPRESSION OR SCREWED FITTINGS – that leak can normally be cured by tightening the nut. Remember with a compression joint to hold the fitting with one spanner whilst you tighten the nut with a second spanner. Do not over tighten the nut – a deformed 'olive' will leak worse than before.

LEAKING CAPILLARY FITTINGS – are more of a problem. **Turn the water off** – drain the pipe by opening taps and using draincocks if necessary. Only when you are certain that there is no water in the offending pipe should you heat and unsolder the joint.

Clean up the pipe and fit a new capillary fitting. Any trace of water inside the pipe will make the joint more difficult to make. A simpler solution may be to cut the pipe either side of the joint and to fit a burst pipe repair compression coupling (see page 26).

PUSH-FIT FITTINGS – should not normally leak, but if it does it is a fairly simple matter to replace it. **Turn the water off** – and drain the pipe, then replace the fitting. Check the instructions with the new push-fit fitting for how to dismantle the old one. Methods vary, depending on the design of the fitting.

INSTALLING A NEW BASIN

A new basin could be a replacement – where the pipework is already in place – or an addition in a bedroom or new cloakroom, where the pipes will have to be installed.

New 15mm copper or plastic supply pipes are connected via compression or capillary tee-fittings to existing pipes. They run to the basin position under the floorboards and along or up walls with clips at regular intervals. Ensure that horizontal pipe runs have a slight fall.

A new 32mm/1¼in plastic waste-pipe must run to and be connected to the main soil stack or – in older systems – the waste hopper. This is not easy with old cast iron systems.

Drill a hole through the wall where the pipe pass through an outside wall. Then open this up from either side with a club hammer and cold chisel.

When buying a basin, remember to buy the taps, waste outlet and trap – make sure the basin has one hole for a mixer and two holes for pillar taps, depending on which installation is being used.

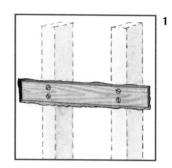

WHEN REPLACING A BASIN – **turn off the water and drain** – before you disconnect and remove the old basin.

WHEN FITTING A NEW BASIN – fit the basin and waste pipe, then – **turn off the water and drain** – to cut into the existing hot and cold water pipes to connect the new supply pipes.

1 Ensure that the wall is strong enough to carry the weight of a wall-hung or pedestal basin.
ON SOLID WALLS – use heavy-duty wall plugs preferably with long reach brass or zinc coated screws.
ON HOLLOW OR PARTITION WALLS – install a batten. To take the weight – this must be screwed directly to the upright studs in the wall. Cut away the plasterboard to install the batten and make good the plaster before fitting the basin.

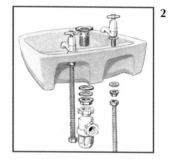

2 Connect the taps before fitting the basin and make sure that the sealing washers provided are correctly fitted.
Connect the waste outlet, this also has a sealing washer.

3 Connect the supply pipes to the basin taps using tap connectors. If you have a modern basin mixer-tap, it may be supplied with 8mm, 12mm or 15mm pipes which will need pipe reduction pieces.
Supply pipes must be connected using compression fittings – to allow removal of the taps in the future.

4 The waste pipe is connected to the plug assembly via a plastic trap – bottle-traps are the neatest.

OPPOSITE: Careful planning will ensure that the style of the bathroom is not compromised by unsightly pipework.

INSTALLING A NEW BATH

2

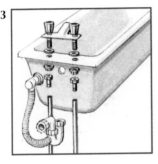

3

Usually a new bath is a replacement so make sure that it will fit into the space and that the size of supply and waste pipe can be routed and adapted to fit the new bath.

1 **Turn the water off** – drain the system. Use a bath/basin spanner to disconnect the supply pipes from the taps.
A cast-iron bath is very heavy. Cover it with a blanket. Smash it with a sledge hammer and remove the pieces.

2 Fit the cradle support to the bath. If the bath is against a solid wall remove a strip of plaster so that the edge can be embedded and rigidly secured into the wall.

3 Run – or extend – the service pipes to new positions. Fit the taps, waste outlet – and overflow link – to the bath. Adjust the legs to level the bath and secure it in position.

4 Connect the waste and supply pipes. Make good the bath surround and seal around the edges with a flexible silicone sealant – to prevent water leakage.

5 Run a 4mm² earth wire from the main earthing point by the consumer unit. Use electrical earth bond connectors fastened to the supply pipes as close to the taps as possible. A metal bath must be earthed.

Elizabeth Whiting Associates

RIGHT:
An old-style bath positioned with a thoroughly modern aspect.

REPLACING AN IMMERSION HEATER

A n immersion heater is like a large kettle element pointing into a hot water cylinder to heat the hot water. It can burn out and will then need replacing.

When buying a new immersion heater, make sure that it is the correct size – 27in for top-fitting heaters and 14in for side-fitting ones – and also that it includes the correct size of thermostat to fit the heater. You will also need an immersion heater spanner.

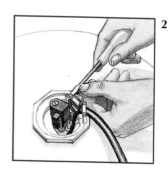

2

1 **Turn off the electricity supply to the circuit** – and close the orange or red handle wheel gatevalve on the cold water supply pipe leading to the bottom of the cylinder.

Attach a hosepipe to the draincock at the bottom of the cylinder and drain it. Drop the other end of the hosepipe into the bath – then open the draincock.

2 Remove the immersion heater cover and disconnect the flex – making a note of where the wires go.

3 Use an immersion heater spanner to unscrew the element, and withdraw it. If the element is stuck – due to scale – use a blowtorch on it.

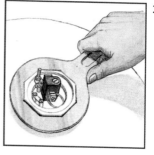

3

4 Wrap PTFE tape around the threads of the new element in a clockwise direction, then insert and tighten it (not too hard) with the spanner.

5 Fit the new thermostat down the centre and wire up the flex. The neutral (blue) wire goes to the heater itself, the live (brown) wire to the thermostat – a link-wire connects the thermostat to the heating element – earth (yellow/green) wire goes to its own terminal.

6 Replace the cover, close the draincock, open the gate-valve and turn on the electricity.

INSTALLING A GARDEN TAP

A garden tap is usually installed on the branch pipe leading to the kitchen cold tap and fitted outside over the same gully as the kitchen sink waste.

1 Start outside by drilling holes to take wall plugs for the screws which secure a wallplate elbow to take the tap. Drill a 16mm/⅝in hole through the wall to take the pipe.

2 Cut a short length of 15mm pipe to run to the hole, then fit an elbow plus a length of pipe though the wall to the inside.

3 Connect the pipe to the wallplate elbow, and fit the wallplate elbow to the wall. Also fit the tap at this stage.

4 Inside, fit an elbow and take more pipe to the position in the branch pipe where you are going to join it. Also fit an in-line valve and a stopcock into the pipe.

5 **Turn the water off** – at the mains stopcock – open the kitchen tap to drain the rising main. Open the draincock and drain off the remaining water.

6 Make two cuts roughly 18mm/¾in apart in the kitchen cold tap branch with a pipe cutter – clean the cut ends of the pipe and fit a 15mm compression tee-fitting to the two old pipes and the new one. Protect pipes against frost – fit waterproof insulation outside.

Running the pipes in this way means that the outside pipe can be drained in winter by closing the stopcock and opening the tap – if you need to run the pipe up to the tap, fit a draincock outside at the corner where the pipe turns.

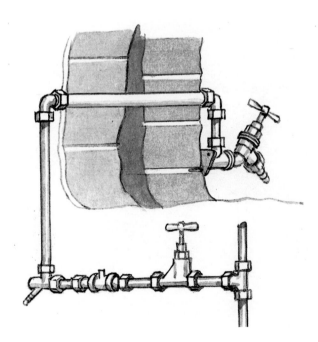

PLUMBING IN A WASHING MACHINE/DISHWASHER

A permanently plumbed in washing machine – or dishwasher – has to be the height of convenience.

Plumbing in

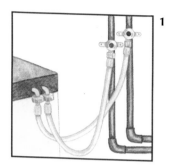

1 **Do not turn the water off.** Use a 'plumbing-in' kit – it has self-cutting valves which fit over the sink supply pipes. When the valve is screwed down it make the connection.
ALTERNATIVELY – **Turn the water off** – and drain the pipe. Cut the supply pipe to insert 15mm compression tee-fittings and run a15mm pipe to the machine position. Fit a mini turn-off valve with ^{3}⁄4in BSP screwed fitting to the end of the pipe and connect the machine supply hose.

Plumbing out

2 CLOSE TO THE SINK – connect the out hose direct to the sink waste pipe with a self-cutting connector.
ALTERNATIVELY – Fit a standpipe to the wall behind the machine with a trap at the bottom. Take the waste pipe from the trap out through the wall to a convenient gully.

2

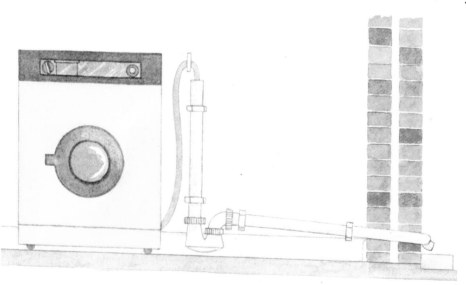

FITTING A NEW COLD WATER CISTERN

If your old cold water cistern is showing signs of serious corrosion – it is time to replace it with a new plastic one. Plastic cisterns come in rigid – rectangular versions, which need a large loft hatch – and flexible – circular versions, which can be squeezed through a hatch.

Make sure you buy a cistern with a capacity of at least 227 litres/50 gallons for a main cold water, or 18 litres/4 gallons for a central heating feed-and-expansion cistern. Buy also a 'Bylaw 30' kit which includes a lid and an insulating jacket.

1 **Turn the water off** – at the mains and drain the cistern – bale out the remains by hand. Disconnect all the old pipes – if it will not pass through the loft hatch, leave it in a corner.

2 The cold water cistern will need a stout platform to support it, resting on at least three loft joists. Ensure all supply pipes are in proper order, and securely clipped in place.

3 Make holes in the tank for the supply pipes in line with the existing supplies so that you will not have to alter these pipes. Modify the rising main, but take the opportunity to fit a 15mm in-line servicing valve and a new tap connector.

Make at least four holes in the cistern.

1 – 21mm hole for Part 2 or 3 diaphragm ballvalve – look for a strong part of the cistern.

2 – 25mm hole to take the plastic tank connector for the 22mm overflow pipe.

3 – two 30mm holes for tank connectors to the 22mm cold supply pipes to feed the bathroom taps, and to feed a hot water cylinder. Both these connections should be made at least 50mm/2in above the base of the cistern – the cold supply to the hot water cylinder should be slightly higher than any cold supply.

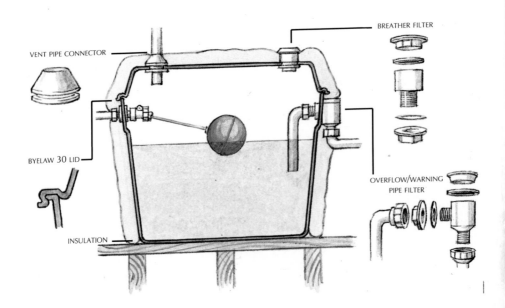

VENT PIPE CONNECTOR

BREATHER FILTER

BYELAW 30 LID

OVERFLOW/WARNING PIPE FILTER

INSULATION

Additional tank connectors will be needed for a power shower or a rim-supply bidet. Both of these must comply with regulations and have their own separate cold supply set in priority order, at water level safety heights to avoid scalding. Get professional advice if in doubt.

Drill any additional holes and then fit the ballvalve – after which turn the water back on.

4 The 'Bylaw 30' kit has a downturn for the overflow pipe, a 'breather' in the lid, a grommet to take the safety open vent pipe (a hole for this should be drilled to match the position of the vent pipe) and an insulating jacket.

5 Run a small amount of water into the bottom of the cylinder to anchor it in place before closing the in-line servicing valve and making all the connections.

6 Fit the insulation jacket once all the connections are completed for the rising mains, cold water feed supply pipes, overflow pipes, jacket vent and breather connections.

FITTING A WATER FILTER

A nxiety about the quality of our drinking water has made fitting a permanent water filter a popular job.

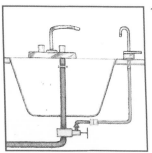

1 The filter is fitted to a bracket secured to the cupboard under the kitchen sink. It is fed from a flexible pipe linked into the branch pipe feeding the kitchen sink cold tap, with a second flexible pipe leading to a new 'tap' mounted in a hole cut in the sink.

2 Drill a 12mm hole in the sink for the tap. Mount the water filter on the under-sink cupboard with screws.

3 **Do not turn the water off.** Connect into the kitchen sink cold water tap branch using a self-cutting valve, fitted over the pipe. Force the pointed cutter into the side of the pipe, allowing water to flow into the filter and into the 'tap'.

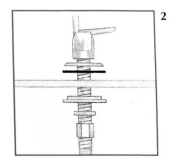

The cartridge in the filter unit lasts for around six months. The tap itself has two positions – down for temporarily on; up for permanently on.

FITTING A BATH/SHOWER MIXER

A bath/shower mixer is the easiest type of shower to fit as it simply replaces the existing bath taps.

The mixer usually has two taps – one hot and one cold – with a diverter lever or knob which allows mixed water to flow either through the spout into the bath or up a flexible hose to a shower-head mounted above the bath.

1 **Turn the water off** – and drain the bath hot and cold taps. Remove the bath side-panel. Use a bath/basin spanner, to unscrew the nut securing the pipe on the nearest tap and then the nut on the furthest tap.

2 Use the spanner to unscrew and remove the taps. Clean off any dried sealing compound on the bath surface.

3 Check that the supply pipes reach the new bath/shower mixer – if short, use an adaptor – and fit the mixer.

4 Drill holes for the shower bracket and fasten to the wall. To comply with Water Bylaws, a restraining ring should be fitted to the bracket or sliding rail to prevent the shower-head from dangling in the bath.

5 Turn on the water to check for leaks – tighten the nuts if necessary – and re-fit the bath panel.

Elizabeth Whiting Associates

INSTALLING AN ELECTRIC SHOWER

Installing an electric shower needs only a cold supply, but you will also have to install a heavy-duty electric circuit from a spare 30A or 45A fuseway in the main consumer unit, which you might prefer to leave to a professional electrician.

If you install the shower in a cubicle in the bathroom or a bedroom, suitable drainage must be installed to the main soil stack. Alternatively an electric shower can be safely installed over the bath, provided that the casing is not in the direct line of spray. All this needs is two or three holes to take wall plugs for the screws to support the shower unit.

1 Run a length of 15mm pipe from the rising main, via a stopcock, to the shower position. Often the easiest place to make the connection is in the loft space, running the (insulated) pipe down through the ceiling to the shower position.

2 **Turn the water off** – and drain through the kitchen taps. Make two cuts 18mm/³⁄4in apart to fit a compression tee-fitting. Clean the cut pipe ends and insert the fitting with the new length of pipe running to the shower.

3 ELECTRICALLY – showers up to 7.2kW need a 30A circuit run in $4mm^2$ cable – $6mm^2$ if the consumer unit has re-wirable fuses or if the cable run is longer than 20m. Showers of more than 7.2kW need a $40A:6mm^2$ or $45A:10mm^2$ cable.

The cable runs to the shower via a ceiling-mounted pull-cord 45A double-pole switch, fitted in the bathroom. The circuit should be RCD (Residual Current Device) protected – if there is no spare fuseway in the consumer unit, an additional switch-fuse unit and a new 'splitter' box will need to be fitted by your local Electricity Company.

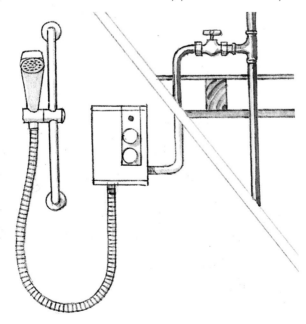

FAR LEFT: A stylish bath shower mixer unit is easy to fit and adds a touch of class to any bathroom.

Made Simple
CENTRAL HEATING

M ost homes these days have some form of central heating already fitted. So the main jobs for the home plumber involve maintaining, improving and updating the present system.

BELOW: Sooner or later old or neglected radiators cease to be as efficient or as capable as we would prefer.

ADDING/MOVING A RADIATOR

Provided the boiler has the capacity, there is usually no problem with adding extra radiators to give more heat.

Replacing an existing radiator with one of greater output – perhaps a double panel for a single panel – has the advantage that the same connections can be used because the radiator is the same length. Sometimes, the radiator just plain has to be moved!

The main problem with adding, moving or replacing a radiator is having to drain down the system – particularly if a corrosion inhibitor has been added. The additive will be lost, and needs to be replaced, if the system is fully drained.

1 **Switch the boiler off and drain the system** – draincocks can be found at the lowest points of the system. Attach a hosepipe to these, leading to outside drains. Start at the top and working downwards, go around the system opening the air bleed valves on radiators (see page 40).

2 To run pipes to a new radiator you will have to cut into the existing flow and return pipes – the flow is the pipe which heats up first when the systems is turned on.

3 Use tee-fittings – reducing tees if joining 15mm pipe to 22mm pipe – so that the pipework goes from the flow to the radiator and then connects to the return pipe.

4 When a radiator is moved, cut through the existing pipes and fit stop-end fittings unless they can be used to extend new pipes to the new radiator position.

5 Fit pipe insulation to all pipes that are under ground-floor floorboards – or where expansion noise is likely (see page 23).

6 When refilling the system, progressively close the air bleed valves as the system fills up. If a new radiator has been added, it should be balanced (see page 40).

3

4

FITTING A THERMOSTATIC RADIATOR VALVE

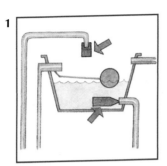

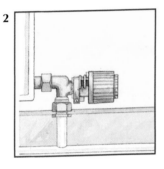

A thermostatic radiator valve reacts to the temperature in the room where it is fitted to reduce or increase the flow through a radiator.

It is a way of saving money on heating costs by limiting the central heating boiler demand in a room that has some other form of heating – a fuel-effect fire or is warmed by the sun during the day.

1 A special kit consisting of two special plugs is available which avoids the need to drain down the system.

One plug is fitted into the cold feed pipe at the point where it leaves the feed-and-expansion cistern in the loft.

The other is fitted over the end of the open vent pipe. The vacuum keeps the water in the system, provided that the radiator valves are removed one at a time – but you will still need cloths to catch any drips.

2 The valve is fitted in place of the existing valve, usually on the 'flow' side of the radiator. Simply disconnect the pipe and unscrew the valve from the radiator.

3 Remove the plugs once the valves are fitted.

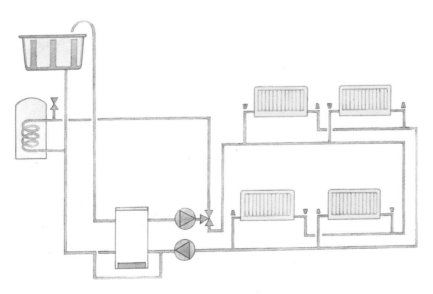

ABOVE: Pumped heating with gravity hot water.

CONVERTING TO FULLY-PUMPED OPERATION

Modern central heating systems are fully pumped – the pump drives water around both the radiator circuit and the circuit which heats the hot water cylinder.

In old systems, only the radiator circuit is pumped, with the hot water circuit relying on 'gravity' circulation. With a fully-pumped system, the hot water will heat up much more quickly and the temperature can be better controlled.

To change gravity circulation to fully-pumped

1 **Switch off the boiler and drain the system** – Reposition the pump after, rather than before, the boiler (see page 44).

2 Remove the flow pipe from the hot water cylinder and disconnect it from the open vent pipe. Leave the open vent pipe in place with a stop-end fitted.

3 In place of the flow pipe, fit a three-way motorised valve after the pump and connect a new flow pipe to the hot water cylinder – insulate the pipe all the way to the cylinder.

4 Fit a cylinder thermostat to the hot water cylinder and wire this to the motorised valve, which in turn is wired back to the programmer, the pump and the boiler.

You will not usually need to reconnect the return pipe from the hot water cylinder to the boiler – check the boiler instructions – but it is essential that the open vent pipe is fitted before the pump.

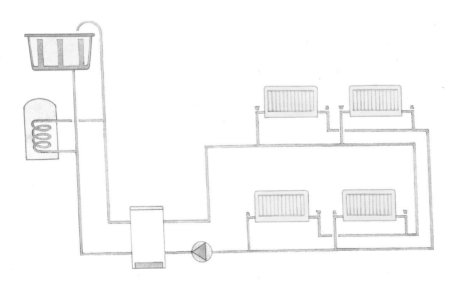

ABOVE: Converted fully pumped operation with pump next to boiler.

Made Simple

REPLACING THE PUMP

Central heating pumps need to be replaced if they fail. If the system was installed correctly – stop-valves are fitted either side of the pump – then this is an easy task.

2

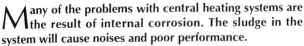

1 **Turn off the electricity supply to the system** – while you disconnect the old pump and connect the new. The electrical connection to the pump are straightforward.

2 **Turn off the stop-valves either side of the pump** – which may need a special handle. The two large nuts either side of the pump can be unscrewed and the pump slid out sideways.

3 Provided the new pump is the same size, it can be slid in, the nuts tightened, and the stopcocks opened.

CORROSION PROTECTION

Many of the problems with central heating systems are the result of internal corrosion. The sludge in the system will cause noises and poor performance.

You can tell whether or not your system has corrosion protection by draining off a jam-jar full from a draincock and leaving a nail in the jar for a couple of days. If it rusts, you have no corrosion inhibitor.

The type of inhibitor needed depends on the type of boiler. The manufacturers of corrosion inhibitor products will be able to tell you which one you should use and also recommend the type of system cleanser you should use beforehand to flush out the sludge in the system.

Instructions are provided – both cleanser and inhibitor are added to the feed-and-expansion cistern in the loft – but you will need to be prepared to drain and refill the system several times.

BLEEDING AND BALANCING RADIATORS

If air gets into the central heating system – or corrosion produces hydrogen gas – the tops of radiators get cold.

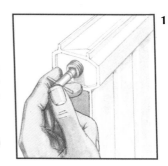

1 Switch the boiler off – Use a radiator key to unscrew the air-bleed screw at the top of the radiator. Allow the air or hydrogen to escape. Hold a cloth under the key to catch any water which comes out when all the air is gone.

You will need to bleed the radiators whenever you drain and refill the system.

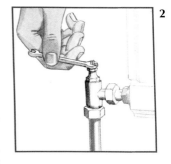

2 With the boiler on – Balance radiators by adjusting the 'lockshield' valve – a free spinning handle – usually fitted on the return pipe. This can be turned with a spanner or by using the handle of the handwheel valve on the flow pipe which should be fully open for balancing.

If a radiator is correctly balanced it has a temperature differential across it of 11°C difference between flow and return. If each radiator is correct then the system is correctly balanced and will distribute heat evenly.

To measure accurately, you will need to buy or hire clip-on pipe thermometers – many plumbers rely on their fingers as temperature-sensing devices.

3 Start with the lockshield fully open and slowly close it until the correct temperature difference is achieved.

REPLACING A BOILER

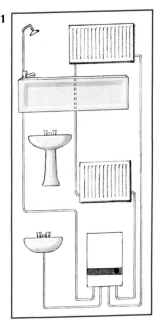

The Gas (Supply and Use) Regulations prohibit you from removing or installing a gas boiler, so this is a job you will have to leave to a qualified gas-fitter.

However, you can decide on the type of boiler installed and make changes to the remainder of the system.

1 Modern gas boilers are more efficient than ever before. A popular choice is a 'condensing' boiler, which costs more but which has a greater efficiency. The 'combination' boiler is also popular, it provides endless instantaneous hot water in addition to central heating.

All new compact 'low water content' boilers need to be installed in a fully-pumped system. Combination boilers are usually installed in a sealed system, where a fill unit and an expansion vessel combine the functions of the feed-and-expansion cistern, which can be removed.

Pipework changes will be necessary to re-route the hot water pipes and to remove the hot water cylinder.

2 Most new boilers will be fitted with a 'balanced flue' – a two-part duct which allows fresh air into the boiler and allows the products of combustion to escape. This does away with the need for a chimney or conventional flue.

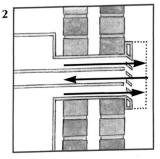

Made Simple
ACKNOWLEDGMENTS

Photography props supplied by:

Nina Barough Styling

As credited, photographic material reproduced by kind permission of:

Elizabeth Whiting Associates